To every thing there is a season,
and a time to every purpose under the heaven:
a time to weep, and . . . a time to mourn.
Ecclestiastes 3:1-4, KJV

May the thoughts gathered in this book
comfort and sustain you during
your time of sorrow.

For

_____

From

_____

A Time to Mourn

Recovering from the Death of a Loved One

Ron DelBene
WITH
Mary & Herb Montgomery

The Upper Room
NASHVILLE, TENNESSEE

A TIME TO MOURN

Cover Transparency: Frances Dorris
Cover and Book Design: Jim Bateman
First Printing: March, 1988 (10)
ISBN 0-8358-0577-8

Printed in the United States of America

Contents

No Sorrow Like Mine

Death has claimed the life of someone you love. Your hurt is so deep and so painful that you sometimes wonder if you will survive your loss. Perhaps you think no one has ever felt sorrow as you are experiencing it. That's a feeling one of our faith ancestors captured when he wrote, "Is it nothing to you, all ye that pass by? Behold, and see if there be any sorrow like unto my sorrow" (Lam. 1:12, KJV).

We all experience love and loss in our own special way. To that extent no one else will experience sorrow exactly the way it is affecting you. But many of the feelings you are having have been felt by others who grieve: feelings of sadness, anger, guilt, shame, uselessness. "Time heals what reason cannot," said the statesman and philosopher Seneca. But from deaths in my own family—as well as my work with others who are grieving—I know that time alone will not heal grief. Overcoming it takes a great deal of effort. We have to acknowledge our feelings and find ways to deal with them. This means accepting the support that others have to give and reaching out for help when that help is not forthcoming.

Also it means turning to God—the God who promises "I am with you always" (Matt. 28:20). At the moment, that promise may have a hollow ring. However, in this difficult and hurtful time you need to accept some things as truth. Look to the scripture that says, "The LORD is near to the broken-hearted, and saves the crushed in spirit" (Psalm 34:18). For now, trust that God knows your pain and will give you the strength to make it from one hour to the next and the courage to face a new day.

Sorrow Comes to Pass, Not Stay

Grief is a natural reaction to loss. It is the acknowledgment that we have lost something of great importance. The loss leaves us with a broken heart. It is through grieving that our spirit mends and our heart is healed.

In my work, I find that those who lack time to mourn lack time to mend. To grieve is to let our emotions run their course instead of fighting them. Denial that something devastating has happened to us merely delays grieving. Years later we may need to relive the experience and express the anguish we suppressed at the time of loss. How poetically and wisely scripture reminds us of the need to deal with our losses as they occur: "To every thing there is a season, and a time to every purpose under the heaven . . . a time to weep, and . . . a time to mourn" (Eccles. 3:1–4, KJV). This is your time to feel pain, your time to look at life and grieve for the ways it has been diminished by the death of someone you loved.

Grief may have taken you so far into the depths that you fear you will never come back. Hard as it may be to believe, you will again be able to smile and be at peace. Some of the most comforting words in scripture are these: "And it came to pass." So it is with grief. For a while you are going to be miserable. But if you work your way through the crying, the loneliness, and the anger, you will find there is life beyond the hurting. As a widow who lost her husband of many years said to me, "After John died, I never thought I'd feel like living again. In time, though, I discovered my grief was like a long, bleak winter. It came to pass, not stay."

A Sign That We Have Loved

One of the great comforts of our faith is that this earthly life is not the end. Jesus tells us: "They who believe in me, though they die, yet shall they live, and whoever lives and believes in me shall never die" (John 11:25–26, adapted). This is a reason to rejoice, but I find it confuses some devout people. The assurance that death is a passing on to a new life with God leaves them feeling their grief is inappropriate. They think that if their faith had real depth they wouldn't hurt so much.

No matter how great our faith, it does not protect us from life's disappointments and sorrows. God created us with feelings, so we are going to feel the pain of separation caused by death. Even God's son was not spared. At the tomb of his good friend Lazarus, "Jesus wept" (John 11:35).

Sometimes a death leaves us so shocked and numb we cannot cry. If the one we mourn died after a lingering illness, we may be left emotionally drained and shed few tears at the time of death. Two months after his elderly mother's funeral, Arthur came to see me. With tears streaming down his face, he said, "This is the first time I've really cried, and I feel like there's no end to the tears."

As the weeks pass, the emotions we hold within need to be released. We may think that by being composed and unemotional, we are symbols of strength to others, particularly if we are the head of a family. In our culture, men especially need to understand that at a time of loss, tears are not a sign of weakness. Rather, they are a sign that we have loved. Expressing this love through tears is the natural and healthy thing to do.

The Angry Feelings

The death of someone we love arouses many emotions. One that can confuse and even frighten us is anger. Feeling angry is a normal part of the grieving process. I have seen anger aimed at a variety of targets. Often it is directed at the deceased for dying and leaving family members with financial worries and burdensome responsibilities.

Even though the survivors know such anger is irrational and unreasonable, they feel it nonetheless. Depending upon the circumstances of the death, anger might be directed at the hospital staff, a doctor, a driver in a fatal crash. Frequently, anger is directed at God. "Why did this have to happen, God?" survivors cry out bitterly. "Why? Why? Why?"

In their angry frame of mind, the grieving feel alone and abandoned by God. That sense of abandonment is something even Jesus expressed. In his final hour on the cross, he cried out, "My God, my God, why hast thou forsaken me?" (Mark 15:34, KJV).

We know that God did not forsake Jesus. Jesus died in order to fulfill a larger plan, a larger purpose. Neither will God forsake any of us in our time of sorrow. God knows our longings, our resentments, our hopes, our despair. However angry we may be, God understands and is with us through the hurtful days and tense, sleepless nights. God is there to comfort, to sustain, and to guide us in finding ways to confront anger and overcome it. Admitting our anger is a first step toward ridding ourselves of this crippling emotion. When we free ourselves of anger, grief will diminish, and joy will again have a place in our lives.

A Need to Talk

I have experienced grief and know it causes feelings to churn. The totally unexpected loss of a friend—a friend who had become like a brother—was an explosion in my life. Some of what I felt found release through tears. Other emotions needed words to give them expression.

I took comfort from talking even more to God in prayer and found myself following my own advice: hold nothing back. God is never shocked or disappointed, loving us as much in our strength as in our weakness, keeping us as close in our despair as in our joy. As the psalmist of old states, "Pour out your heart before him; God is a refuge for us" (Psalm 62:8).

If in this hurtful time you don't feel God's love directly, remember that it is often revealed through the care and compassion of others. Friends want to help but often don't know how. If help is not forthcoming, it is important to reach out and ask for what you need. Very possibly what you need most is someone to talk to. When a couple's infant daughter died, the young mother recognized their need for help and called me. "We can't handle this alone," she had told her husband. "We need to find someone who will let us talk and listen to our feelings."

To whom should you talk? It might be to a trusted friend, a clergy person, or members of a grief support group. Depending upon the degree of your remorse and anger, you may want to seek the help of a professional counselor. Most of us have a great need to share our ordeal. We need to talk until we have exhausted words and can see for ourselves the steps necessary to move beyond grief.

_ With Forgiveness Comes Peace _

When someone dies, we have a tendency to focus on what we *could* have done or *should* have done. Perhaps we even think we could have prevented the death if we had gotten an earlier diagnosis or hadn't let the person drive or had recognized the warning signs that seem so clear afterward. Our regrets tend to make us angry with ourselves, and anger directed at self becomes guilt.

I have found that the most effective way to be rid of guilt is to confide in someone I trust. By revealing the torments of the heart, we come to see that most of our regrets are not grounded in reality. In looking back, we are reminded of the many caring, loving things we did for the person we mourn. We are then able to focus less and less on what we did not do.

In this time of remorse and regret, it is well to remember the parable Jesus told of the prodigal child who comes home to a forgiving parent. In telling that story, Jesus shows us that the parent had forgiven the child before the child said anything. If we feel in need of forgiveness and seek it, we can know that God has already forgiven us and embraced us in love. God will also grant us the grace to forgive ourselves for wrongs both real and imagined.

There is an old Greek saying that goes, "It takes charity to forgive someone else. It takes wisdom to forgive ourselves." With God's help we can grow in charity and in wisdom so that we might forgive others and forgive ourselves as well. Then we come to know peace of mind and heart.

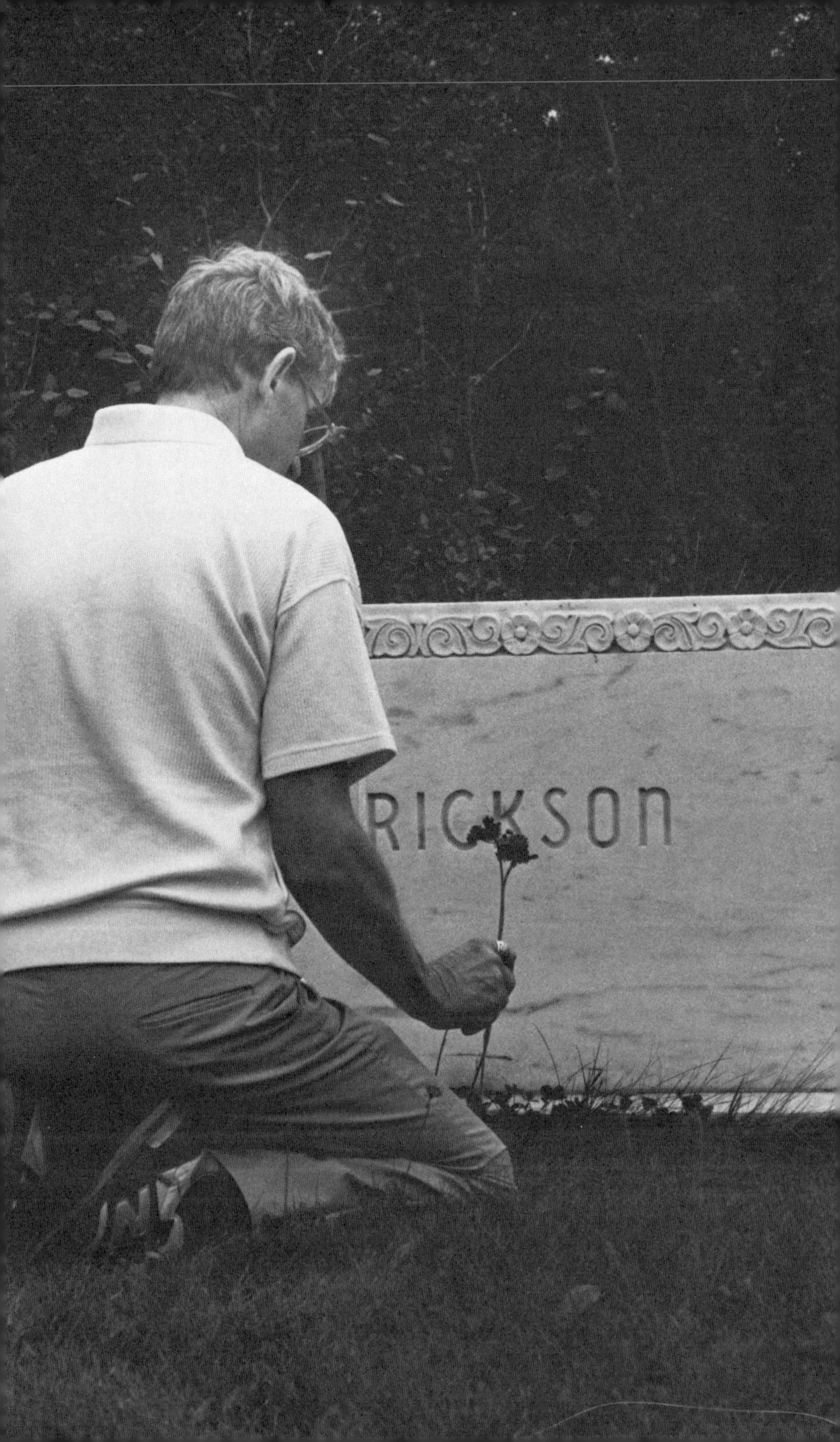
RICKSON

Through the Valley
Of the Shadow

Only those who have lost someone they love know how long grieving lasts. After the death of a family member or close friend, it can easily be eighteen to twenty-four months before we feel in charge of our emotions. If the death was a violent one, it can take even longer. The good friend I mentioned earlier died more than three years ago. Though I have mainly fond memories now, I still feel occasional moments of deep sadness.

Many people tell me they were in a state of shock at the time of death and only later felt the full impact of their loss. The low point tends to come in about six months. Depression may then force us into a dark valley—a valley from which there seems no way out.

This is not the time to put up a brave front. When people ask how we're doing, we shouldn't always say "fine." We need to let a few supportive friends know how miserable we are and reach out to them for comfort. We can also find comfort as well as hope in the psalm that speaks of the Shepherd who knows our sorrows and will lead us out of the valley:

> The LORD is my shepherd; I shall not want. He maketh me to lie down in green pastures: he leadeth me beside the still waters. He restoreth my soul: he leadeth me in the paths of righteousness for his name's sake. Yea, though I walk through the valley of the shadow of death, I will fear no evil: for thou art

with me; thy rod and thy staff they comfort me. Thou preparest a table before me in the presence of mine enemies: thou anointest my head with oil; my cup runneth over. Surely goodness and mercy shall follow me all the days of my life: and I will dwell in the house of the LORD for ever.

—Psalm 23, KJV

One Day at a Time

Past hurts naturally lead us into worry about the future. Such was the case with Joan, a widow with young children to raise. "What will tomorrow bring?" she asked me worriedly. "If more sorrow comes, will I be able to handle it?"

I reminded Joan that when questions about the future were put to Jesus, he said, "Do not be anxious about tomorrow, for tomorrow will be anxious for itself. Let the day's own trouble be sufficient for the day" (Matt. 6:34). Jesus' message to Joan—and to all who grieve—is to live one day at a time.

However difficult something may be, we can endure it for twenty-four hours. By making it through one day, we gain the confidence to make it through another. And another. Of course there will be days when we are filled with anxiety, days when our courage falters, days when we think we can't go on. But we can go on, and we will make it through our grief.

We have only so much capacity to carry sorrow, and eventually grieving ends. In the process, we gain inner strength and gather new resources for living. But no matter how satisfactorily we work through our grief, we never get completely over the loss of someone we love. Memories of what was and thoughts of what might have been will always bring a bit of sadness. The melancholy is most likely to overtake us on holidays, anniversaries, and other days that have special meaning for us. But those days of sadness—like all days—come one at a time. Like a dark cloud, the sadness passes. Once again light and laughter come into our lives.

_ A Return of Purpose and Meaning _

I believe there comes a point when we need to understand that the best memorial to a loved one is a full and _growing_ life. It is a time when we should look not so much at what we have lost but at what we have left.

Those we hold dear never really leave us. They live on in the kindnesses they showed, the happiness they shared, and the love they gave. Although life without that special person will never be the same, we can still find purpose and gladness in our days. I find it important to remember that with God all things are possible. With God's steadfast support, we can banish fear and doubt. With God's healing power, we can take the broken pieces of our lives and fit them into something new and useful.

When we stop focusing exclusively on our own hurt, we are overcoming grief. When we look around and see that there are people with needs we can fill, we are moving back into the mainstream of life. What we do doesn't have to be anything major. It might be inviting someone for a meal or writing a letter of condolence. It might be caring for someone's plant or pet or child.

I saw this change clearly in George whose son died in a car accident. I didn't see George for a long time after our many talks. Then I got a letter from him. "One day," he wrote, "I reached out to a neighbor who needed an ear to listen and realized I'd turned a corner in my life."

Reaching out to help others brings purpose and meaning to our days. Once more we come to appreciate that life is a gift from God and that each day is made special by how we accept it and the love with which we live it.

Pursuing New Dreams

After suffering the death of someone we love and experiencing the anguish of loss, questions arise. Is it all just a hurtful, negative experience? Or will something positive come of it?

Scripture tells us: "We know that all things work together for good to them that love God" (Rom. 8:28, kjv). But what good will come of the pain? How can something positive come from the loss of one we hold dear?

Of itself, our suffering has no value. Good will come of it only if we give meaning to the experience of loss—only if we are determined to use the experience to grow. Over and over I have seen an increased capacity for tenderness and a new awareness of the suffering of others grow out of emotional pain.

Through the experience of loss, I discovered inner strengths I didn't know I had. And so will you. As you confront your grief and work through the pain, you will gain the confidence necessary to fashion a new life.

Jesus tells us: "Behold, I have set before you an open door" (Rev. 3:8). What door has opened for you? Possibly you will want to start a new career, become active in church, volunteer for programs in the community, return to school, or engage in any number of activities that provide new challenges and lead you down new paths.

As believers in a merciful, loving God, you and I are called to leave our fears behind. We are to pursue new dreams. In doing so, we will find joy in the present and know that with God's help our future is unfolding as it should.

The Prayer Within

When someone we love dies, we long to feel God's comforting presence. Yet in this time when we need God so much, we are likely to find that God seems distant and remote. Although we may have found peace and comfort in prayer before, even that does not seem to help now. As a grieving mother said to me after her son's death, "Praying is just too hard at the moment." And a husband who had lost a wife of many years confided, "After Ellen died, I was so numb I couldn't even remember prayers I'd been saying for years. When I finally was able to pray, the prayers seemed so shallow. They weren't expressing what was in my heart and helping me feel close to God."

In this time of anguish, I find there is a simple way to pray that speaks from the heart and lets us feel the nearness of God. It is not a prayer that uses other people's words. Rather, it is a short, personal prayer that lies within each of us, a prayer we discover for ourselves. Known as the breath prayer, it comes as easily and naturally as breathing and reminds us that we share the breath of God. Saying the prayer lets us know that we are not alone in the midst of the pain and confusion grief brings. God is there to comfort, guide, and sustain us.

To discover your breath prayer, follow these five easy steps:

Step One

Sit in as comfortable a position as possible. Then be calm and quiet. Close your eyes and remind yourself that God loves you and that you are in God's loving presence.

Recall a favorite passage from scripture that places you in the proper frame of mind. "Be still, and know that I am God" (Psalm 46:10) is a line people often find helpful.

Step Two

As you keep your eyes closed, imagine that God is calling you by name. Listen carefully and hear God asking you: "(*Your name*), what do you want?

Step Three

Answer God with whatever comes honestly from your heart. Your answer may be a single word, such as *peace* or *love* or *forgiveness.* Your answer may instead be a phrase or brief sentence, such as "I want to feel your forgiveness" or "I want to understand your love" or "I want to be with you." Whatever your response is, it becomes the heart of your prayer.

Step Four

Choose your favorite name for God. (Choices people commonly make include God, Jesus, Christ, Lord, Spirit, Shepherd, Creator.)

Step Five

Combine your name for God with your answer to God's question "What do you want?" and you have your prayer. For example:

What I Want	Name I call God	Possible Prayer
peace	God	Let me know your peace, O God.
love	Jesus	Jesus, let me feel your love.
rest	Shepherd	My Shepherd, let me rest in thee.

What do you do if several ideas occur? You need to eliminate or combine ideas until you have focused your prayer. You may "want" many things. But if you think carefully, you can narrow your wants to a specific need that you feel is basic to your well-being. When you have gotten to the heart of your needs, search for words that give it expression. Then work with the words until you have a prayer of six to eight syllables. The words should flow smoothly whether spoken aloud or expressed silently as heart-thoughts.

Your prayer may be most rhythmic when God's name is placed at the beginning, but try it at the end as well. One way will feel better than another. When your prayer seems right for you, write it down. Then use it throughout the day. You can whisper it. You can say it aloud. You can think it. Some people use "triggers" to help them remember to say their prayer: whenever the phone rings, during radio or TV commercials, when sitting down to eat. Also use it when you go to bed or wake up at night or during lonely times when you want to be more aware of God's nearness.

Because the prayer can be said so effortlessly, it enables us to follow the apostle Paul's call to "pray without ceasing" (1 Thess. 5:17, KJV). In Paul's letter to the Romans he says, "Be patient in tribulation, be constant in prayer" (Rom. 12:12). Likewise in his letter to the Ephesians he tells us: "Pray at all times in the Spirit, with all prayer and supplication" (Eph. 6:18). And in yet another letter we are reminded to "continue steadfastly in prayer" (Col. 4:2).

The breath prayer is a way to be constant in prayer and to feel a oneness with God. This ancient way of praying takes its name from the Hebrew word *ruach*. The word can be translated as "wind," "breath," or "spirit." It is the *ruach* of God that is breathed into all living beings. Even when you are not consciously praying, the words of the breath prayer will play in your heart and help ease the pain of your grief.

This is my breath prayer:

Peace I leave with you; my peace I give it to you; not as the world gives do I give to you. Let not your hearts be troubled, neither let them be afraid.

—John 14:27